TIME IS MONEY

Because time is money
and YOUR time (and money)
is valuable!

Published by BOLD publishing
Copyright 2019 by BOLDpublishing
All Rights Reserved

By Deena Cunningham

THIS BOOK BELONGS TO:

_____

"There is no substitute for hard work. Never give up. Never stop believing. Never stop fighting "-
Hope Hicks

TIME IS MONEY

PAY PERIOD: _____ - _____

DATE	START TIME	BREAK (TOTAL)	LUNCH TO-FROM	BREAK (TOTAL)	FINISH TIME
			-		
			-		
			-		
			-		
			-		
			-		
			-		

TOTAL REG. HOURS

TOTAL O.T. HOURS

DAYS
ABSENT

NOTES

TIME IS MONEY

PAY PERIOD: -

DATE	START TIME	BREAK (TOTAL)	LUNCH TO-FROM	BREAK (TOTAL)	FINISH TIME
			-		
			-		
			-		
			-		
			-		
			-		
			-		

TOTAL REG. HOURS

TOTAL O.T. HOURS

DAYS
ABSENT

NOTES

TIME IS MONEY

PAY PERIOD: —

DATE	START TIME	BREAK (TOTAL)	LUNCH TO-FROM	BREAK (TOTAL)	FINISH TIME
			—		
			—		
			—		
			—		
			—		
			—		
			—		

TOTAL REG. HOURS

TOTAL O.T. HOURS

DAYS
ABSENT

NOTES

TIME IS MONEY

PAY PERIOD: ‑

DATE	START TIME	BREAK (TOTAL)	LUNCH TO-FROM	BREAK (TOTAL)	FINISH TIME
			‑		
			‑		
			‑		
			‑		
			‑		
			‑		
			‑		

TOTAL REG. HOURS
TOTAL O.T. HOURS

DAYS
ABSENT

NOTES

TIME IS MONEY

PAY PERIOD: ‎ —

DATE	START TIME	BREAK (TOTAL)	LUNCH TO-FROM	BREAK (TOTAL)	FINISH TIME
			—		
			—		
			—		
			—		
			—		
			—		
			—		

TOTAL REG. HOURS

TOTAL O.T. HOURS

DAYS ABSENT

NOTES

TIME IS MONEY

PAY PERIOD: ‎ -

DATE	START TIME	BREAK (TOTAL)	LUNCH TO-FROM	BREAK (TOTAL)	FINISH TIME
			—		
			—		
			—		
			—		
			—		
			—		
			—		

```
TOTAL
REG. HOURS

TOTAL
O.T. HOURS
```

DAYS
ABSENT

NOTES

TIME IS MONEY

PAY PERIOD: _____ - _____

DATE	START TIME	BREAK (TOTAL)	LUNCH TO-FROM	BREAK (TOTAL)	FINISH TIME
			—		
			—		
			—		
			—		
			—		
			—		
			—		

TOTAL REG. HOURS

TOTAL O.T. HOURS

DAYS
ABSENT

NOTES

TIME IS MONEY

PAY PERIOD: _____ - _____

DATE	START TIME	BREAK (TOTAL)	LUNCH TO-FROM	BREAK (TOTAL)	FINISH TIME
			—		
			—		
			—		
			—		
			—		
			—		
			—		

TOTAL REG. HOURS

TOTAL O.T. HOURS

DAYS ABSENT

NOTES

TIME IS MONEY

PAY PERIOD: -

DATE	START TIME	BREAK (TOTAL)	LUNCH TO-FROM	BREAK (TOTAL)	FINISH TIME
			-		
			-		
			-		
			-		
			-		
			-		

TOTAL REG. HOURS
TOTAL O.T. HOURS

DAYS
ABSENT

NOTES

TIME IS MONEY

PAY PERIOD: —

DATE	START TIME	BREAK (TOTAL)	LUNCH TO-FROM	BREAK (TOTAL)	FINISH TIME
			—		
			—		
			—		
			—		
			—		
			—		
			—		

TOTAL REG. HOURS

TOTAL O.T. HOURS

DAYS ABSENT	NOTES

TIME IS MONEY

PAY PERIOD: —

DATE	START TIME	BREAK (TOTAL)	LUNCH TO-FROM	BREAK (TOTAL)	FINISH TIME
			—		
			—		
			—		
			—		
			—		
			—		
			—		

TOTAL REG. HOURS

TOTAL O.T. HOURS

DAYS
ABSENT

NOTES

TIME IS MONEY

PAY PERIOD: —

DATE	START TIME	BREAK (TOTAL)	LUNCH TO-FROM	BREAK (TOTAL)	FINISH TIME
			—		
			—		
			—		
			—		
			—		
			—		
			—		

TOTAL REG. HOURS

TOTAL O.T. HOURS

DAYS
ABSENT

NOTES

TIME IS MONEY

PAY PERIOD: -

DATE	START TIME	BREAK (TOTAL)	LUNCH TO-FROM	BREAK (TOTAL)	FINISH TIME
			-		
			-		
			-		
			-		
			-		
			-		

TOTAL REG. HOURS

TOTAL O.T. HOURS

DAYS
ABSENT

NOTES

TIME IS MONEY

PAY PERIOD: —

DATE	START TIME	BREAK (TOTAL)	LUNCH TO-FROM	BREAK (TOTAL)	FINISH TIME
			—		
			—		
			—		
			—		
			—		
			—		
			—		

TOTAL REG. HOURS

TOTAL O.T. HOURS

DAYS ABSENT

NOTES

TIME IS MONEY

PAY PERIOD: -

DATE	START TIME	BREAK (TOTAL)	LUNCH TO-FROM	BREAK (TOTAL)	FINISH TIME
			-		
			-		
			-		
			-		
			-		
			-		
			-		

TOTAL REG. HOURS
TOTAL O.T. HOURS

DAYS
ABSENT

NOTES

TIME IS MONEY

PAY PERIOD: _____ - _____

DATE	START TIME	BREAK (TOTAL)	LUNCH TO-FROM	BREAK (TOTAL)	FINISH TIME
			-		
			-		
			-		
			-		
			-		
			-		
			-		

TOTAL REG. HOURS

TOTAL O.T. HOURS

DAYS
ABSENT

NOTES

TIME IS MONEY

PAY PERIOD: –

DATE	START TIME	BREAK (TOTAL)	LUNCH TO-FROM	BREAK (TOTAL)	FINISH TIME
			–		
			–		
			–		
			–		
			–		
			–		
			–		

TOTAL REG. HOURS

TOTAL O.T. HOURS

DAYS
ABSENT

NOTES

TIME IS MONEY

PAY PERIOD: —

DATE	START TIME	BREAK (TOTAL)	LUNCH TO-FROM	BREAK (TOTAL)	FINISH TIME
			—		
			—		
			—		
			—		
			—		
			—		
			—		

TOTAL REG. HOURS
TOTAL O.T. HOURS

DAYS
ABSENT

NOTES

_____
_____
_____
_____
_____
_____
_____
_____
_____
_____
_____
_____

TIME IS MONEY

PAY PERIOD: _____ - _____

DATE	START TIME	BREAK (TOTAL)	LUNCH TO-FROM	BREAK (TOTAL)	FINISH TIME
			–		
			–		
			–		
			–		
			–		
			–		
			–		

TOTAL REG. HOURS

TOTAL O.T. HOURS

DAYS
ABSENT

NOTES

TIME IS MONEY

PAY PERIOD: ‎ ‎ ‎ –

DATE	START TIME	BREAK (TOTAL)	LUNCH TO-FROM	BREAK (TOTAL)	FINISH TIME
			–		
			–		
			–		
			–		
			–		
			–		
			–		

TOTAL REG. HOURS

TOTAL O.T. HOURS

DAYS
ABSENT

NOTES

TIME IS MONEY

PAY PERIOD: -

DATE	START TIME	BREAK (TOTAL)	LUNCH TO-FROM	BREAK (TOTAL)	FINISH TIME
			-		
			-		
			-		
			-		
			-		
			-		
			-		

TOTAL REG. HOURS
TOTAL O.T. HOURS

DAYS
ABSENT

NOTES

TIME IS MONEY

PAY PERIOD: _____ - _____

DATE	START TIME	BREAK (TOTAL)	LUNCH TO-FROM	BREAK (TOTAL)	FINISH TIME
			—		
			—		
			—		
			—		
			—		
			—		

TOTAL REG. HOURS

TOTAL O.T. HOURS

DAYS ABSENT

NOTES

TIME IS MONEY

PAY PERIOD: ‌ ‌ ‌ ‌ —

DATE	START TIME	BREAK (TOTAL)	LUNCH TO-FROM	BREAK (TOTAL)	FINISH TIME
			—		
			—		
			—		
			—		
			—		
			—		
			—		

TOTAL REG. HOURS
TOTAL O.T. HOURS

DAYS
ABSENT

NOTES

TIME IS MONEY

PAY PERIOD: ‐

DATE	START TIME	BREAK (TOTAL)	LUNCH TO-FROM	BREAK (TOTAL)	FINISH TIME
			‐		
			‐		
			‐		
			‐		
			‐		
			‐		
			‐		

TOTAL REG. HOURS

TOTAL O.T. HOURS

DAYS
ABSENT

NOTES

TIME IS MONEY

PAY PERIOD: _____ - _____

DATE	START TIME	BREAK (TOTAL)	LUNCH TO-FROM	BREAK (TOTAL)	FINISH TIME
			–		
			–		
			–		
			–		
			–		
			–		
			–		

TOTAL REG. HOURS

TOTAL O.T. HOURS

DAYS
ABSENT

NOTES

TIME IS MONEY

PAY PERIOD: ‐

DATE	START TIME	BREAK (TOTAL)	LUNCH TO-FROM	BREAK (TOTAL)	FINISH TIME
			‐		
			‐		
			‐		
			‐		
			‐		
			‐		

TOTAL REG. HOURS

TOTAL O.T. HOURS

DAYS
ABSENT

NOTES

TIME IS MONEY

PAY PERIOD: –

DATE	START TIME	BREAK (TOTAL)	LUNCH TO-FROM	BREAK (TOTAL)	FINISH TIME
			–		
			–		
			–		
			–		
			–		
			–		
			–		

TOTAL REG. HOURS
TOTAL O.T. HOURS

DAYS
ABSENT

NOTES

TIME IS MONEY

PAY PERIOD: —

DATE	START TIME	BREAK (TOTAL)	LUNCH TO-FROM	BREAK (TOTAL)	FINISH TIME
			—		
			—		
			—		
			—		
			—		
			—		
			—		

TOTAL REG. HOURS

TOTAL O.T. HOURS

DAYS
ABSENT

NOTES

TIME IS MONEY

PAY PERIOD: ‑

DATE	START TIME	BREAK (TOTAL)	LUNCH TO-FROM	BREAK (TOTAL)	FINISH TIME
			‑		
			‑		
			‑		
			‑		
			‑		
			‑		
			‑		

TOTAL REG. HOURS

TOTAL O.T. HOURS

DAYS
ABSENT

NOTES

TIME IS MONEY

PAY PERIOD: —

DATE	START TIME	BREAK (TOTAL)	LUNCH TO-FROM	BREAK (TOTAL)	FINISH TIME
			—		
			—		
			—		
			—		
			—		
			—		
			—		

TOTAL REG. HOURS

TOTAL O.T. HOURS

DAYS
ABSENT

NOTES

TIME IS MONEY

PAY PERIOD: –

DATE	START TIME	BREAK (TOTAL)	LUNCH TO-FROM	BREAK (TOTAL)	FINISH TIME
			–		
			–		
			–		
			–		
			–		
			–		
			–		

TOTAL REG. HOURS

TOTAL O.T. HOURS

DAYS
ABSENT

NOTES

TIME IS MONEY

PAY PERIOD: -

DATE	START TIME	BREAK (TOTAL)	LUNCH TO-FROM	BREAK (TOTAL)	FINISH TIME
			-		
			-		
			-		
			-		
			-		
			-		
			-		

TOTAL REG. HOURS

TOTAL O.T. HOURS

DAYS
ABSENT

NOTES

TIME IS MONEY

PAY PERIOD: —

DATE	START TIME	BREAK (TOTAL)	LUNCH TO-FROM	BREAK (TOTAL)	FINISH TIME
			—		
			—		
			—		
			—		
			—		
			—		
			—		

TOTAL REG. HOURS

TOTAL O.T. HOURS

DAYS
ABSENT

NOTES

TIME IS MONEY

PAY PERIOD: ‑

DATE	START TIME	BREAK (TOTAL)	LUNCH TO-FROM	BREAK (TOTAL)	FINISH TIME
			‑		
			‑		
			‑		
			‑		
			‑		
			‑		
			‑		

TOTAL REG. HOURS

TOTAL O.T. HOURS

DAYS ABSENT

NOTES

TIME IS MONEY

PAY PERIOD: –

DATE	START TIME	BREAK (TOTAL)	LUNCH TO-FROM	BREAK (TOTAL)	FINISH TIME
			–		
			–		
			–		
			–		
			–		
			–		
			–		

TOTAL REG. HOURS

TOTAL O.T. HOURS

DAYS
ABSENT

NOTES

TIME IS MONEY

PAY PERIOD: ‑

DATE	START TIME	BREAK (TOTAL)	LUNCH TO-FROM	BREAK (TOTAL)	FINISH TIME
			‑		
			‑		
			‑		
			‑		
			‑		
			‑		
			‑		

TOTAL REG. HOURS
TOTAL O.T. HOURS

DAYS ABSENT

NOTES

TIME IS MONEY

PAY PERIOD: _____ - _____

DATE	START TIME	BREAK (TOTAL)	LUNCH TO-FROM	BREAK (TOTAL)	FINISH TIME
			—		
			—		
			—		
			—		
			—		
			—		
			—		

TOTAL REG. HOURS

TOTAL O.T. HOURS

DAYS
ABSENT

NOTES

TIME IS MONEY

PAY PERIOD: —

DATE	START TIME	BREAK (TOTAL)	LUNCH TO-FROM	BREAK (TOTAL)	FINISH TIME
			—		
			—		
			—		
			—		
			—		
			—		
			—		

TOTAL REG. HOURS

TOTAL O.T. HOURS

DAYS
ABSENT

NOTES

TIME IS MONEY

PAY PERIOD: ‐

DATE	START TIME	BREAK (TOTAL)	LUNCH TO-FROM	BREAK (TOTAL)	FINISH TIME
			‐		
			‐		
			‐		
			‐		
			‐		
			‐		
			‐		

TOTAL REG. HOURS
TOTAL O.T. HOURS

DAYS
ABSENT

NOTES

TIME IS MONEY

PAY PERIOD: –

DATE	START TIME	BREAK (TOTAL)	LUNCH TO-FROM	BREAK (TOTAL)	FINISH TIME
			–		
			–		
			–		
			–		
			–		
			–		
			–		

TOTAL REG. HOURS
TOTAL O.T. HOURS

DAYS
ABSENT

NOTES

TIME IS MONEY

PAY PERIOD: _____ - _____

DATE	START TIME	BREAK (TOTAL)	LUNCH TO-FROM	BREAK (TOTAL)	FINISH TIME
			–		
			–		
			–		
			–		
			–		
			–		
			–		

TOTAL REG. HOURS

TOTAL O.T. HOURS

DAYS
ABSENT

NOTES

TIME IS MONEY

PAY PERIOD: —

DATE	START TIME	BREAK (TOTAL)	LUNCH TO-FROM	BREAK (TOTAL)	FINISH TIME
			—		
			—		
			—		
			—		
			—		
			—		
			—		

TOTAL REG. HOURS

TOTAL O.T. HOURS

DAYS
ABSENT

NOTES

TIME IS MONEY

PAY PERIOD: —

DATE	START TIME	BREAK (TOTAL)	LUNCH TO-FROM	BREAK (TOTAL)	FINISH TIME
			—		
			—		
			—		
			—		
			—		
			—		
			—		

TOTAL REG. HOURS

TOTAL O.T. HOURS

DAYS
ABSENT

NOTES

TIME IS MONEY

PAY PERIOD: _____ - _____

DATE	START TIME	BREAK (TOTAL)	LUNCH TO-FROM	BREAK (TOTAL)	FINISH TIME
			—		
			—		
			—		
			—		
			—		
			—		
			—		

TOTAL REG. HOURS

TOTAL O.T. HOURS

DAYS
ABSENT

NOTES

TIME IS MONEY

PAY PERIOD: –

DATE	START TIME	BREAK (TOTAL)	LUNCH TO-FROM	BREAK (TOTAL)	FINISH TIME
			–		
			–		
			–		
			–		
			–		
			–		
			–		

TOTAL REG. HOURS

TOTAL O.T. HOURS

DAYS
ABSENT

NOTES

TIME IS MONEY

PAY PERIOD: ‎ ‎ ‎ ‎ ‎ ‎ ‎ ‎ ‎ ‎ ‎ -

DATE	START TIME	BREAK (TOTAL)	LUNCH TO-FROM	BREAK (TOTAL)	FINISH TIME
			—		
			—		
			—		
			—		
			—		
			—		

TOTAL REG. HOURS

TOTAL O.T. HOURS

DAYS
ABSENT

NOTES

TIME IS MONEY

PAY PERIOD: -

DATE	START TIME	BREAK (TOTAL)	LUNCH TO-FROM	BREAK (TOTAL)	FINISH TIME
			-		
			-		
			-		
			-		
			-		
			-		
			-		

TOTAL REG. HOURS
TOTAL O.T. HOURS

DAYS
ABSENT

NOTES

TIME IS MONEY

PAY PERIOD: −

DATE	START TIME	BREAK (TOTAL)	LUNCH TO-FROM	BREAK (TOTAL)	FINISH TIME
			−		
			−		
			−		
			−		
			−		
			−		

TOTAL REG. HOURS

TOTAL O.T. HOURS

DAYS
ABSENT

NOTES

TIME IS MONEY

PAY PERIOD: -

DATE	START TIME	BREAK (TOTAL)	LUNCH TO-FROM	BREAK (TOTAL)	FINISH TIME
			-		
			-		
			-		
			-		
			-		
			-		
			-		

TOTAL REG. HOURS
TOTAL O.T. HOURS

TIME IS MONEY

PAY PERIOD: —

DATE	START TIME	BREAK (TOTAL)	LUNCH TO-FROM	BREAK (TOTAL)	FINISH TIME
			—		
			—		
			—		
			—		
			—		
			—		
			—		

TOTAL REG. HOURS
TOTAL O.T. HOURS

www.ingramcontent.com/pod-product-compliance
Lightning Source LLC
Chambersburg PA
CBHW070431220526
45466CB00004B/1635